How Can I Raise Eagles When I'm Just another Turkey?

Stories, Essays, & Ramblings of an ADHD PHD Teacher/Missionary

by

P. Mark Taylor

Koinonia Associates LLC
Clinton, TN

How Can I Raise Eagles When I'm Just another Turkey?

ISBN   978-1-60658-002-8

Koinonia Associates LLC
Box 763
Clinton, TN 37717

To learn how you can become a published author, visit
http://www.PublishWithKA.com

100% of the author royalties
will be donated to
Eagle's Nest Christian Academy, Inc.,
a nonprofit organization in Heiskell, TN.

The mission of *Eagle's Nest* is to develop and
provide programs, ministries, and facilities that
provide a supportive and educational Christian
environment for children in need.

Faith through Love
Excellence through Hope
Leadership through Service

www.eaglesnestkids.org

Contents

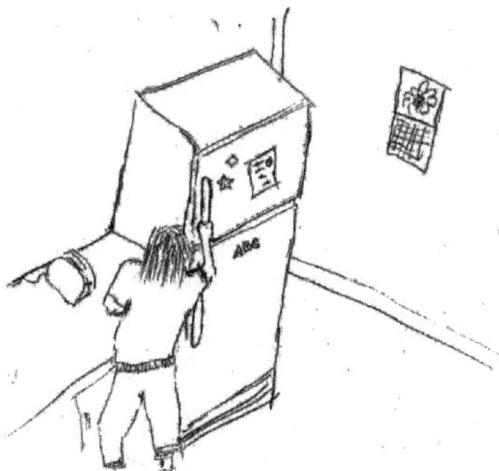

EYEGLASSES IN THE FREEZER

A few months into our first adoption, my wife Karen awoke one morning and stepped downstairs to begin the day. As with every day, she started by picking up her reading glasses from the place she had left them the night before. She could see reasonably well without them, but she would get a headache if she started reading. She expected to find them somewhere in the kitchen, so she marched into the room and checked every surface twice. No reading glasses. She went to the other spots where she might have taken them off: the bathroom, in front of the television, her dresser. After an exhaustive search Karen could not find her eyeglasses anywhere.

Finally, it struck her: Ask Katlin! Katlin is our youngest daughter and at that time, we were in the process of adopting her along with her brother and sister. While she is truly a gift straight from God, we realized almost immediately that this child was gifted: she could make a mess out of anything! Katlin had been described by her new second grade teacher as a tornado. "She leaves a path of destruction and disarray in her wake."

When Karen found Katlin doing what she does best down in the basement. We had a fantastic play room down there with many activities that had many parts – the ideal place for a cute little tornado to hang out and make messes. Karen cleared her throat as she entered the room and immediately had her attention. "Katlin, do you know where my glasses are?"

Without missing a beat, Katlin hurried to the kitchen and pulled Karen's reading glasses out of the freezer. Amused and very curious, she had to find out the rest of the story:

Karen: "Why were my reading glasses in the freezer?"

Katlin: "When I opened the freezer to look for frozen waffles this morning, your glasses fell out. I remembered what you said about putting things back from where we got them, so I put them back in the freezer."

After several minutes of uncontrolled laughter, Karen kindly explained to Katlin that she had put her reading glasses on top of the refrigerator and not inside the freezer. When Katlin had flung the freezer door open, the way that tornados do, it must have been jarred loose and fallen down. She was sure to finish with praise for Katlin's willingness to put things back from where she got them.

Her perspective on eyeglasses and freezers must have been different from ours. Katlin's unique perspective on many things in life can sometimes be a burden, but often it is refreshing. The event must have made quite a large impression because Katlin has rarely followed the rule since that day!

HOW FAMILIES WORK

Not long after coming into our home, Anthony, our newly adopted eleven year old son, had a fight with Jake. Jake is the older of the two boys born to us. For over 10 years, Jake had been the oldest child in the family and used to ruling the roost. It was inevitable that there would be conflict. Both boys came down the stairs upset and found me at the dining room table. Jake started to explain that Anthony had been choking him. Knowing better than to assume the worst, I probed for further information.

They had been fighting over toys that they had traded. After a few deals, they did not agree as to who owned a particular toy and had a heated discussion. After living in some tough situations and living in seven different foster homes before coming to us, Anthony knew how to fight. As it turns out, however, Jake is the one who lost his temper first and pushed Anthony. It was clear to me that he had followed the rule that police are trained to follow, using the least harmful means possible to get the perpetrator to stop. In this case, the perpetrator was his new brother.

We do have rules against fighting back, however, and I started in on my lecture. "Jesus said to turn the other cheek and that is what we expect. Jake was wrong, but you were wrong, too." Before I had a chance to make a ruling and dole out justice to both of them, Anthony dropped his head low, turned, and started walking out of the kitchen. Standing up to gain his attention I blurted out, "Where are you going?" Anthony turned towards me and looked up.

His eyes were watering. He raised his quivering voice in frustration and forced out the words: "I'm going upstairs to pack. That's what happens every time we get in trouble!"

We were the eighth placement in the foster care system for Anthony and his two sisters. Each home lasted less than three months and most of the time they had to leave because the parents could not handle their behavior. They had been placed in a home for adoption right after Thanksgiving of the previous year, but the "parents" had returned them to the state of Tennessee on December 24th. They had lots of Christmas presents and no family. After two years of moving from home to home, Anthony had no reason to expect any different from us.

It must have been God speaking through me in the moment because what came out of my mouth was more profound than anything I had ever said before or have said since: "Families don't work that way. When there is a problem, we deal with it and keep going." His shoulders dropped as he relaxed. That was the day that Anthony decided that it might be okay to stop being a father to his sisters. That was the day that he began to relax and just be their brother, because now they had a Dad.

BUMPING CUPS

The neediness of our new children was especially challenging during the initial months and years of adoption. They would poke and prod her for constant attention. For months the girls asked, "Who do you love more, me or my sister?" This was not with their words, mind you, but with their actions. They wanted us to pick who should get the love and who would be left out. Similarly, all of the children struggled to find their place in the family. We explained to them many times that, "God has placed you in our family and God is love. Therefore, He has placed in our heart a full measure of love for each of you. Each of you has the same amount, whether you were born into the family or adopted into the family."

Beyond this, was the question: When does love end?" With her behavior, Katlin kept asking the question: "If I do this, will you still love me?" On the one hand, she really wanted to be kicked out of every family, so that the department of Children's Services would be forced to return her to her mother. As irrational as that sounds, she believed it and put it into action on a regular basis. On the other hand, however, she desperately needed to know that somebody loved her regardless of her behavior – unconditionally.

This began to wear on me, but it was killing my wife. Karen is the most loving, caring, compassionate, Christian woman on the face of the planet. Our kids and I truly believe it. Still, they would not cut her a break. They could not understand that every human has to have a break. If you continually demand attention and ask these emotional questions, eventually even the most wonderful person will snap. Our children just didn't get it. Even our birth children could not understand this. Finally, I came up with a way to communicate these ideas and an important spiritual truth, all in one lesson. I rounded up all of the children and had them sit at the kitchen table. On the table, I placed a large plastic bowl, a stack of Styrofoam cups, and a pitcher of water.

"God is love," I explained, "and all throughout the Bible God is represented by water. When we are baptized in water, we are filled with the Holy Spirit, who is God. "

I then filled one cup. Holding it over the large bowl, I poked a whole in the side of the cup.

"Since Adam and Eve sinned, we live in a fallen world. That means we have a hole in our cup. Since we became Christians, the holes in our cup are sealed. Still, the world will get to us once in a while and bump our cups." I reached up and slapped the cup just enough to spill some water.

"Some people do a better job holding their water than others. Mom is pretty good at it. Moreover, she goes to God and gets refilled through prayer and praise." I topped off Moms leaky cup once more.

Then, I addressed the problem in our household: "You guys have been running around with cups that are mostly empty. That feels yucky. You want water and you should. Without water, we would die. You want water, but instead of getting it from the true source, God, you have been trying to get it from each other and from Mom. You have been bumping cups!" At this point I, had each of the children hold a cup over the bowl. I filled the cup that represented Mom, grabbed another cup and bumped it to knock some water out of Mom's and into the other cup.

Immediately, they understood the cup-bumping game and several tried to bump Mom's cup in order to fill theirs. Within a few seconds, there was water everywhere and very little in anyone's cup.

"Who has enough water to be okay?"

"Nobody," they answered.

"That's right. When you bump other people's cups, they lose water and you never get enough. "

"How do we get enough water, then?", asked Madison.

"Well, there are two ways to get it," I replied. You can wait for Mom to pour water into your cup, or you can go directly to the source and get some. Either way, however, you have to hold your own cup steady and accept the gift of water in order to receive water. Forcing someone to love you is like bumping cups. It will always leave you wanting more and always hurt the other person."

With that, I had them all follow me to the kitchen sink. When we had all gathered around the sink, I turned it on and held Mom's cup under it.

"Now put your cups under Mom's and try not to bump anyone else's cup." After a little jostling, they managed to find a spot where they could constantly keep their cup full.

"This is how we are all going to be okay at the same time. There is enough love to go around; we just have to accept the love we are given instead of bumping cups to try to get it. Now please stop bumping each other to be okay... ***AND***... stop demanding Mom's attention. With God, there is always enough love. Mom wants to fill your cups, but you have to wait for her and allow her to receive it from God. When you demand it on cue, both you and Mom end up empty and miserable."

.

ADVICE FOR A FUTURE
PREACHER

For the last few years, I have had the privilege of mentoring a young man who wants to be preacher when he grows up.

I took him aside one day and asked about his prayer life:

P. Mark:	"How much do you pray each day?
Young Man:	"I pray three times a day."
P. Mark:	"How many minutes does that total up to on the average day?" I followed.
Young Man:	"About five minutes total each day, I guess," he responded with a quizzical look on his face.
P. Mark:	What would you think about a preacher that only prayed five minutes each day?"
Young Man:	"Oh."

That was a great insight for him, but I heard the message loud and clear as well.

- Who was I to challenge this young man's relationship with God?
- How much time have I been praying?

As with every instance of effective teaching, the teacher had learned as much as the student. It was time for a change.

I JUST DON'T SEE WHAT YOU
SEE...

It was a moment worthy of the parenting hall of fame! For the one-billionth time, my daughter and I were butting heads. She was undergoing the usual transformation for a teenage girl preparing for a date: putting on way too much make-up and not nearly enough clothing. (Can I get an AMEN from the Fathers in the room?)

So many times, we had gone over the concepts involved:

- "Looking beautiful and looking sexy are two completely different things."
- "The kind of attention that that brings is not the kind of attention that fills your cup." (See the chapter for Bumping Cups)
- "I'm not making you change to make you miserable; I am having you dress in ways consistent with your stated goals and values."
- "The more skin that shows, the less he will be interested in getting to know you."

She tried her usual arguments:

- "It's the style. This isn't sexy, this is just normal."
- "I am just trying to look nice and nothing else fits me."
- "I don't feel good in anything else. This is my favorite outfit."

To tell you the truth, I melt just a little bit on that last argument. I really do want my daughters to feel special when they dress up for a date or special occasion. I just don't want them to be treated

21

poorly because of the way they dress. I want young men to treat my daughters with respect.

In this moment, my daughter was clearly way over the line. She knew it and I knew it. Finally, she pulled the last weapon out of her arsenal – crying. It might have gotten me to give in a little bit, but then she let slip those words that I will always cherish:

"I just don't see what you see!"

My darling daughter got that deer-in-the-headlights look when she realized what she had said. At the same time, my stern look had faded into the biggest grin I have ever had.

"I didn't mean to say that," she stuttered.

"I know, but you did say it. And you are right. You don't see what I see. That is why we are fighting. When you do see what I see, you will make different choices. It's called growing up. When you see what I see, I will not have to check your outfit anymore because you will choose your attire wisely."

Soundly defeated and feeling a little silly, she marched up the stairs to her room to pick out a more appropriate outfit. ☺

LESSON LEARNED

** An Excerpt from <u>Fast Food Education</u>. See Final Chapter.

Sally was an average student. I knew that she was capable of thinking but was a reluctant participant in my Algebra 2 class. To be specific, Sally seemed to be most concerned with:

- Surviving high school
- Making sure her make-up and hair were just right
- Talking to her friends
- Avoiding speaking in class

More poignantly, Sally did not expect to understand the mathematics we were doing. She was merely hanging on to enough of it to escape with a low C.

On the last day of school, when the teaching and finals were all done, we were sitting around talking. Sally was relaxed and talking openly in a way that she had not done since the beginning of the school year. She turned her head a little and looked at me with an open and honest comment that cut me to the very core of my being: "Remember the first day of class when we did that lab with the bouncing balls? Yeah, I thought this class was going to be different." Ouch! I thought I had been different. I thought that I was doing a great job and I was a teacher that they could rely on to help them be ready for college and the rest of their lives but... BLAM! There it was. I had been revealed for the well-intended fraud that I was.

You see, on the first day of Algebra 2, I had the students working in groups of four. Each group was to drop a rubber ball and record the number of bounces. For each height we tried, they dropped the ball twice and counted the number of bounces. They recorded the average of the two for each height in an x-y table of values. Of course the balls were bouncing everywhere.

At times it looked a lot more like recess at a pre-school than an organized, purposeful lesson in an Algebra 2 class. Much of the time, the students needed more than two drops from a height for various reasons: the students counting were not ready, they were not sure that they had dropped it from the right height, ... but after one day of ball dropping and a second day of graphing and analyzing the results, they had learned. They understood from the results of dropping balls that not everything comes out to be linear. They understood that there were experiences in their lives that could be explained and predicted through higher mathematics. They also understood that mathematics learning did not have to be boring.

Sally had learned this lesson well enough to know that we had spent the remainder of the year doing the drudgery of lecture and practice when there was a way that was more fun AND, more importantly, more meaningful. Sally's comment on the last day of Algebra 2 hit the nail on the head. While I had managed to teach many children a lot of mathematics, this unmotivated student had been more insightful and reflective than any comment that I had managed to utter during that school year.

A TURKEY IN AN EAGLE'S NEST

I have made so many mistakes, blunders, miscues, and bad decisions in my life. It is a wonder that I have not been killed or imprisoned by now. No, I am not quite as bad as that might sound, but truly, most of the people that I know are in the same boat. So many mistakes, so little time.

I started out a quiet underachieving child, in the slow reading group in first grade. I eventually became interested in mathematics, muddled through high school with a B average and escaped four years of college with a degree in mathematics. If my undergraduate performance was lackluster, my social skills left even more to be desired. I will not burden you with the vast majority of details of the mistakes and just plain bad decisions that I made early in life. It suffices to say that my academic and social problems were compounded by a lack of spiritual growth. This dynamic combination made my early career very challenging. When I started looking for a job as a mathematics teacher, there was a shortage of mathematics teachers. Still, I struggled and ended up with part-time jobs for a couple of years. My miscues as an undergraduate also hurt when I decided to further my education. If not for a solid GRE score, I would not have been accepted into a masters degree program at all. As it was, I entered into graduate school on academic probation. I became a mathematics teacher, but still, so I had trouble finding a full-time teaching job.

Still, the Lord *is* good and He has blessed me. Certainly the greatest of these blessings is my wife. The daughter of missionary and seminary professor, Karen knew a lot more about God than I did. She still does, but thanks to her influence I have learned an incredible amount. He blessed me with my wife Karen as I was completing a masters degree. At that point, things began to improve. I managed to secure a job teaching mathematics in a small high school. During the three years at that job, Karen and I were blessed with the birth of two boys. After three years of teaching, five fundraising projects, one prom, creating a math club, and the tearful graduation of the class of 1996, I felt that I had conquered teaching in the conventional manner. Five years and a lot of life lessons later, I had earned a PhD in curriculum and instruction. For the next seven years, I served as a teacher educator, carrying the title of assistant professor for six years and associate professor for one more year at the University of Tennessee. During these seven years, we adopted four children and learned an incredible amount about God, served in various roles in churches, and even took a few courses in the masters program at Johnson Bible College.

Despite the new self that I have managed to put on, I would still rate myself as more of a turkey than an eagle. I still struggle with my social skills, still suffer through the temptations which are common to men, and I still worry too much. Despite earning turkey status, the Lord has called me to His service, to minister to children. Specifically, I am called to help eagles - those young people that have great potential but are living in homes where and where they are unlikely to find the support they need to become the Christian leaders that they have the potential to become. In effect, the job is to identify eagles growing up in turkeys' nests and transplant them to a new home where they will get everything they need to become Christian leaders – a true eagle's nest.

The question that I have at this point seems obvious, given the trail of miscues of the past as well as my ongoing struggles: How can I raise eagles when I am just another turkey?

On the first day of the Leadership Anderson County class, we had to introduce ourselves with our first name and adjective that starts with the same letter of the alphabet that fits our lives. I was *Missionary Mark*. It still feels uncomfortable. If they only knew how bad I have been, the mistakes I have made. What a turkey! Thankfully, we Christians are seen by God as being covered by the holy blood of Jesus, our sin-stained bodies look white as snow. Otherwise, He wouldn't have anything to do with me, even now that I have cleaned up my act. But He forgives. All have sinned and fall short of the glory of God, but from this collection of sinners he still appoints preachers, teachers, and leaders.

I am unfit to represent the Lord in any way, but he still chooses to forgive and he still gives me assignments. How does the story of my life qualify me to develop and run a children's home, especially an eagle's nest? I do understand the idea of being an underachiever. It is really only in the last decade that I have managed to redirect that. I also know what it feels like to have sense of being powerless, as these children no-doubt feel. I also know what it feels like when things actually take a turn for the better – to begin to have hope. I started with no social skills and made it up to mentoring individuals and leading groups as a regular part of life. In my adult life, I started as a loner and ended up heading a large family, most of whom are not biologically

31

related to me. Moreover, I started out *knowing about God* and have begun to *know God* as Lord, master, and friend. As a result of these changes, I understand that morals, social responsibility, leadership, and spiritual growth are all things that can be learned and taught. As I look at it that way, perhaps a recovering turkey such as me might be able to do some good. With the Lord as my shepherd, all things are possible.

I know I have rambled and there are some missing details, but there it is. I am an unworthy missionary sent to serve children - to raise other people's children and help them become Christian leaders.

ONE HOUR LIST [PART A]

Mary Kay called me from her office one day to ask a favor. Mary Kay was the director of field placements for the preservice teachers in our programs at the University of Tennessee. As another portion of her work, however, she was in charge of the Lyndhurst Elementary Program, which allowed people to have their mid-life crisis to crunch a lot of teacher education courses in the summer so that they can do their internship (student teaching) in the fall. Mary Kay was leading a team of folks, mostly doctoral students, that would serve as the UT supervisor for several some of the Lyndhurst Elementary cohort.

"Can you visit with the folks on the team and tell us what we should be looking for in a math lesson?"

Now, I am a math guy, so I should be excited about the fact that they want to know, right? Well, yes. Sort of. That was my first reaction and I gave her a hearty, "Sure. I'd be glad to talk to the team." Upon hanging up, however, I was overwhelmed. "Do they really expect me to tell them in one hour what it has taken me an entire doctoral program to learn?" That is, after all, what Mary Kay was asking for – a one hour doctoral program – the bulleted version of my professional brain. "Wow!" I thought. "How am I supposed to meet that challenge in a way that will be meaningful and not put them down as being ignorant?"

Don't get me wrong. These are intelligent, gifted people, all of whom had experience teaching, just not math teaching. Gosh, even if they had math teaching experience that is not enough to "get" what they should be looking for in a math lesson. I actually research how mathematics teachers learn and this can't be done. Yet, since I had agreed to do it, I plowed forward. I had to start with the obvious question: What matters more than anything else?

With that question in mind, it was not difficult to brainstorm a short list of critical ideas. That list still encompasses most of the basics of mathematics teaching. That really was the best I could have done at this early stage in my career as a professor of mathematics education. The trick was in figuring out how to help them truly understand the items on the list. I walked into that meeting sure that this was the best one hour presentation of mathematics teaching that I could put together. I'm not sure how much stuck with them, but I know that I learned a lot from that challenge.

The first lesson that I learned was to major on the majors. In other words, it taught me how to prioritize what I teach in my courses. Only teach that which is important. We don't have time to do it all well, so pick what is important and give it the proper portion of attention. Second, it taught me that people don't get what we do - even if they are in a very related field - even if it within your field. They did not know it but they asked me to pour out my heart and soul – my very being in that hour. That was the last lesson. If it can be summarized in one hour, then maybe I shouldn't be treating it as if it were a life-or-death matter. Every once in a while, I look back and laugh at myself and how critical I had made it out to be.

So why should it matter to you that this one hour occurred? What can you glean from this experience? Simple. Majoring on the majors, a focus on what really matters and giving it its proper level of time and energy takes three things:

1)   Decide what is actually important.

2) Decide what can be done with the resources at hand (including time).
3) Decide that other things do not matter.

Jesus faced this dilemma. He had His orders from the Father: "Good job living up until now but go get yourself caught, let them beat and ridicule you, and then, in a day or two from now, die on the cross as a common criminal." When Jesus knew His time on earth was short, He taught like crazy. He gathered His closest disciples and tried to impart everything they would need to know in that time. Unfortunately, the disciples didn't always "get" what Jesus was saying. Even after three years of hanging out with Him as He taught and being His right hand helpers, they did not understand much of what He was saying. This fact was not lost on the greatest teacher to ever walk the planet. He knew that teaching only the most important things and nothing else, there was a chance that they would eventually understand. As such, Jesus taught the twelve disciples about the coming of the Holy Spirit and the roles that the Spirit would do. Jesus taught about the horrors that He would have to endure and the suffering that they would have to do in order to continue following Him.

ONE HOUR LIST [PART B]

The one hour experience made me think. If I knew that I was going to die later today, what would I want to tell my children about life in the precious little time I had left? So here it comes: my one hour list. It is what I want my kids to know when they leave our home. Nope. Scratch that. It is what I want my kids to BE when they leave, grow up, and move on from our home. I changed from "know" to "be" in that sentence because knowing is not enough. Living life right demands acting in accordance with what you know is right. Whatever you act out, that is what you are. Since I want to be a good role model, the chapters of this book represent goals that I am working towards as well. This is what I want to become because it is what I want for my kids. What about you? What are the most important lessons in your life? What should the priorities, habits, and beliefs of the modern-day Christian be?

My One-Hour List

1. Be God's children.
2. Be warriors.
3. Be learners.
4. Be servants.
5. Be leaders.

I want my kids to be God's children. In the first year after adopting three of our children, a sibling group, my wife was asking the question, "When are they going to act like they are my kids?" What she meant was, when are they going to align themselves with my way of thinking and do what they are supposed to?" You see, they are not really ours until they act like it. Sometimes our biological children act in ways that are not consistent with the way we had taught them up to that point. During those times, they were not being our kids. In the Old Testament, the Israelites were referred to as God's children, but they often chose to ignore that and sometimes acted out. Most of the time, actually; they were pretty naughty. I want to tell my kids what it means for any of us to be God's child, including the notions of holiness/purity and seeking Christ-likeness.

I want my kids to be warriors. Male or female, they should be either preparing for battle or engaged in one. Not a battle for themselves, mind you, but soldiers in the army of God. Jesus said that "you are either for me or against me," light or dark. You make the choice. Even if you have chosen to not decide, you have still chosen the dark because you have not sought the light. Furthermore, it is not just a matter of picking sides but engaging in battle for the side you choose. The Old Testament is full of actual battles that the Lord asked His people to fight. The New Testament is full of imagery from war that describes the spiritual battle that we are continuously engaged in, whether consciously or not. I want to use my last moments to help my kids understand what it means to be a warrior on God's side.

I want my kids to be learners. For my dissertation, I interviewed over fifty mathematics teachers in varying stages of life. By the end of the interviews, this one critical attribute of what makes a teacher great stood out among the rest. I soon realized that there are two kinds of teachers that have been doing the job for thirty years; those that have thirty years of experience and those that have one year of experience thirty times. Likewise, I have seen teachers in their first few years of teaching that have packed many years of experience in just a few years. Learners are excited about what they do. Learners get better at what they do. Their energy is contagious. I want my kids to become unstoppable, contagious learners.

I want my kids to be servants. When our first child was born, he was a heaping pile of neediness and self-centeredness. He would scream out things that were nothing like words but we knew what he was saying, "I want food! Get this stuff out of my diaper!" You see, when humans are born they think only about themselves and their survival. As they grow physically, emotionally, and spiritually, they are supposed to developing a sense of other – the idea that other people have needs that they might be able to meet and that this could be a good thing. So good, in fact, that they might actually want to give up something in order to help them. I want my kids to proactively model what it means to be servants, proactively loving others.

I want my kids to be leaders. Let's face it. Not everybody hears God or for that matter not everyone is even trying to listen. Nonetheless, we are in this thing together and we need to act like it. Pulling people together and getting them on track takes everything we covered in the first four bullets: seeking to please God, listening and obeying Him, constantly learning, and seeking the good of others. Beyond these, however, leaders have a special something that enables them to hold it all together while the world around them is in chaos. Moreover, I want my kids to continually be renewed and filled with the Spirit, the key to effective leadership that does not fold under pressure.

Here comes the toughest part. Since I first thought about it and wrote them down, I am trying to lead by example, to become what I want for my children. The list is short and simple. It has to be. We don't get that much time on earth. Stay focused and you will bring God glory. Stay focused on what God wants from you and when you get to the finish line, He will say, "Well done, good and faithful servant."

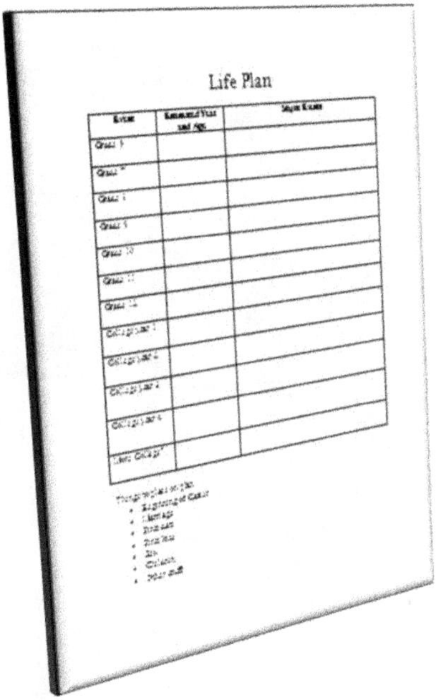

LIFE PLAN

Another great parenting joy is the timely use of a tool we call a *Life Plan*. A Life Plan is simply a timeline with some of the biggest and most important events of your life on it. Having my teenage children map out their life has turned out to be the best argument I have ever come up with. I suppose I should say that it is not a tool for arguing as much as a tool for getting myself out of the line of fire when my kids want to have more freedom to make poor decisions.

The first time that the Life Plan really worked well was when my daughter was, for the millionth time, telling us what she was going to do when she graduated from high school. The problem was that there were far more things in her plan than one could do in a lifetime. I tried to convince her to make some decisions amongst all of those choices, but she thought I was being ridiculous – just another old person that didn't really get it. Man, I hate that!

Anyway, I went to the computer and printed up a piece of paper with years marked down the left side. I asked her to go into the other room and write in every major thing she wanted to do next to the years that she wanted to do them. She took the piece of paper into the next room and carefully thought things through. I have to say that I thoroughly enjoyed the experience. I was not in the room with her, but I was close enough to hear her gasps. I was close enough to hear as she repeatedly said to herself, "Oh!" When she came back to the room that I had been patiently, albeit gleefully, waiting, she had a different attitude. She actually wanted my advice on how to focus her plan!

The next great victory brought on by the Life Plan was with one our sons. He was ANGRY. He didn't think it was right. He was 15 years old and I was telling him what he could and could not do with his girlfriend. On his behalf, I should tell you that I am very conservative when it comes to dating. I can't imagine a teenager that would not be frustrated with my rules. IF you are mature enough and trustworthy enough, then:

- You can group-date at 14 – supervised by a parent that I trust.
- You can go on a regular date when you are 15, provided that it is closely supervised by a parent that I trust.
- During those first two stages, you will not touch or even lean in to get close.

Perhaps the most challenging of my rules is that last one and all of the rules of touch that follow. Back to the story, my son had a BIG issue with touch. He wanted to hug – a regular, face-to-face, two-arm hug. He was angry that it was not allowed and his body language was shouting at me – "I will not treat you with any sort of respect until you let me do what I want!" When I hit a brick wall like this with my children, I know it is time to break out the life plan. It is the right tool for a moment like this because I make the rules for them and not for myself. Their behavior helps or hurts their lives now and in the future. As a parent, a former teenager, and a human being with four decades of life experience, I understand more about life and love than my teenagers. I don't know it all, but I know more than them. Do not, however, try that argument with them in the moment of their frustration. To them, you are just proving the point that you don't get it and you never will.

Anyway, I saw the moment for a Life Plan had come. I handed him a piece of paper with a blank timeline and marked his graduation year. Then, I asked him a series of questions as we filled out the plan:

- Are you going to college?
- What year will you be done?
- When do you plan to be married?
- When are you planning to start having sex? I would like for it to be when you get married but that is not up to me.

Thankfully, he put sex and marriage on the same place in the timeline. ☺ I followed this momentous decision with the following little speech:

"Now comes the tough decision-making: What comes between now and then? Just like Dr. Dobson told us, (a reference to the "Preparing for Adolescence" trip a year or two earlier) there are stages of touch. With every stage, it gets more and more difficult to slow down and wait before the next stage. We get excited when we first hold hands, but that excitement fades after a while and we want that excitement again so we move on to the next stage of touch without even thinking. Soon, we have gone way too far. You have set a goal of waiting until you are married. If that is your goal, then what stages should we put down on this paper and when in this timeline we put them. If you make a good plan and stick to it, then I will not need to tell you what you can and cannot do."

With that, I was telling him that I wanted to hand control over his life to him, especially his love life. Just like handing him the keys to the car when he turned 16, the keys would be taken away when he was not acting responsibly. I did not say that I would stop insisting that his dates be supervised by a parent. In our family, unsupervised dating starts during the senior year of high school. What I did give him, however, was absolutely critical. I shifted the primary responsibility for major life-impacting decisions from me to him. As long as he was doing a good job with those decisions, I would respect those decisions. The act of supervising dates is not about me telling what he cannot do, but it is about me supporting him in his decisions – assisting him with reminders of his goals, his decisions, and helping him keep on track to meet his goals.

FAMILY STANDARDS

"You want us to do what? That stinks!" This is the response each time I get really organized and made a checklist of behaviors for my kids to follow. They know all too well that their privileges are tied with their behavior, but in my first attempts there were two things they did not like about these systems. The first thing they did not like was my tendency to only rate their behaviors when something went wrong. That meant that they were unlikely to keep all of their privileges. Second, it meant that they would get lectured on how well they were not doing. As a matter of fact, these things are great teaching tools because it gives you a way to communicate your core values. At the beginning of our large-family experience, however, we were just trying to manage basic everyday things.

Let's take a look at one of my early attempts at setting objective standards:

	1 Excellent	2 Good	3 Bad
Attitude about Cleanliness			
Attitude towards School			
Attitude at Bedtime			
Attitude about Eating			
Loving Others			
Morning Routine			
Obeying Mom & Dad **the first time!**			

7-10 points = Special Hour with Dad (on another day)
11-14 points = Normal – nothing happens
15-16 points = 1 hour time out
17-18 points = all day time out

53

I am not going to tell you what happened at 19 or above, but I will say that at least one of my lovely children was a frequent flier at that altitude! On a positive note, when they earned the "special hour with Dad" we did some cool things like eating popcorn while we watched a video, going to the park, or playing tag. The worst negative of this system, however, is that it teaches the wrong idea about love. It is not something that is earned. They should have special time with Dad regardless of their behavior – unconditional love. Hence, even the most positive part of the scheme had a negative side.

After several such systems, my passion for trying new systems waned and I put it on the back burner. Periodically, I would have to make up a new rule for a new and interesting behavior. Moreover, the more time we spent without a "system" in place, the more the kids began to see me as the bad guy. When they felt like watching television instead of cleaning, I had to play the tough guy who made them march to their room. When they broke a rule or pushed the limits as far as they could, I was the one that had to get them to back down. I was the one standing between them and what they wanted to do. I had become the enemy.

There was no question; I had to return to a system. The question was of what kind of system would work well for behavior, for teaching them values, and for making the battle between their desires and reality instead of between them and me. The resulting system seems to work pretty good at all three purposes (so far). You might recognize the headings as they are covered in this book. They represent the five topics from my one-hour list.

This was an easy decision because I had already put so much effort into determining that list before, this truly represented my priorities. Why teach anything that is not a top priority? Why discipline for anything that is not of lasting consequence?

Be God's Children	
	Studies Bible **Daily** before or after school
	Prays independently for 15 minutes daily
Be Warriors	
	Proactively seeks to do God's Will **without being told** This includes: • Obeying standing orders such as obey your parents and love others • Listening for special projects He might want you to do
	Prioritizes family/team/group over self This includes: • Looking for and doing special projects that will help the family/group/team
Be Learners	
	Focuses on learning throughout the school day AND outside of school This includes: • Doing all homework as thoroughly as possible and seeking to fill any zeroes that might show up on Edline as soon as you possibly can • Studying even when you think you will do well
	Reflects on learning **and looks for ways to improve** This includes: • Changing the way (how and how much) you study and/or do homework until you _**consistently**_ earn "A"s on <u>tests</u> (and overall)
Be Servants	
	Prioritizes cleanliness **and** excellence over fun This includes: • If it is not clean, clean it (room, house, yard, body, pets) (It does not matter whose job it is or what is on TV) • Chores, studying, and all other areas in this table are **complete** (not just "done") before using computer, phone, ipod, or internet
	Exemplifies humility in all situations and with all people • Seek to serve other people • Listening more than you speak • Rarely bring attention to yourself and your achievements
Be Leaders	
	Tries to be the hardest worker in any group
	Encourages others through a positive tone **and** words of affirmation

One particularly tricky aspect of establishing the Taylor Family Standards was seeing how everything fit into those broad categories. Where does "clean your room" fit into these? I had also been looking

Each category (10 goals) will be scored periodically as:
- Needs Improvement (+0)
- Trying with a good attitude(+1)
- Doing well (+2)
- Wow (+3)

Deal-Breakers
- **Each act of disrespect will receive a (-3) on current score AND count in the ratings for the next score.**
  - Disrespect towards anyone – parents, teachers, siblings, peers, ...
  - Saying "just joking" does not erase the disrespect
- **Each act of dishonesty will result in immediate loss of all privileges for one day.**
  This includes:
  - lying, lies of omission, or deception of any kind
  - trying to find a way around the rules
- **Each act of defiance or danger will result in immediate loss drop to black level for a minimum of 3 days.**
  This includes:
  - Not following orders from authority immediately and appropriately
    (parent, teacher, or older sibling when appropriate)
  - Violence towards people or animals
  - Endangering self or others
  - Crossing moral boundaries
    - *dressing immodestly (showing cleavage or underclothes, ...)*
    - *sexual/sensual behavior inappropriate for age/stage of lifeplan)*

Levels and Privileges	
Only Jesus would score a 30.	
Blue Ribbon (20 and above)	unlimited television 1 hour computer 1 hour video games 1 hour phone dating privileges (as Dad determines) overnight visits and/or after school study group (periodically)
Green Ribbon (15-19)	unlimited television ½ hour computer ½ hour video games ½ hour phone dating privileges (as Dad determines) overnight visits and/or after school study group (periodically)
Yellow Ribbon (10-14)	2 hours television ½ hour video games 15 minutes phone No dating privileges overnight visits and/or after school study group (periodically)
Red Ribbon (5-9)	1 hour television ½ hour video games 5 minutes phone *(timed by a parent – no parent, no phone)* No dating privileges No overnight visits or after school study group
Black Ribbon (4 & below)	Grounded in room No phone, video games, ipod, computer, or TV

for a way to fit leadership lesson into our everyday lives. How would I fit that into this scheme? How do I fit every detail into the scheme without varying from my five priorities AND have few enough rules to actually be practical. That is a lot to do in a document that I wanted to fit on one 8½ by 11 page.

Finally, I had to establish a positive scoring system. It had have a gradual increase in privileges. The system had to have important privileges like the phone at a very achievable level, while not giving full privileges to kids that are not trying to do well. I started out at the top level – full privileges. To determine what score it would require I simply started with by thinking about my kids that do not get in trouble and usually try hard and do well. Unless something weird is going on, they should retain full privileges. So I set the score of 20 as the lowest score for full privileges. If you are giving a good effort at everything, there is no reason you should not be able to retain all privileges. Looking at the more unpredictable end of the behavior spectrum, to have any privileges a child should at least try and not cop an attitude. That set the score for the first privilege level at 5. From there it was just a matter of filling in the details and an emergency plan for when something really goes wrong.

As I said, it has worked well so far. Then again, parenting is never a done deal. If you are not constantly learning of your own free will and accord, your children will most certainly teach you a lesson that you never wanted to learn. Hence, take the "Taylor Family Standards" as a work in progress. Do not try to copy it. Copy instead, the process. Set your priorities, focus on the positives, and get ready for the negatives.

I MISS BEE TAG!

When the kids where younger – ages 8, 9, 10, 11, and 12 – we would play bee tag. Bee tag is a simple game. It is playing tag with a bee. Not a real bee, of course, but a stuffed bee. Kind of like a bean bag with yellow and black stripes.

The main floor of our house was a continuous loop. You could run VERY fast through the kitchen, study/dining room, the family room, the dean, the eat-in kitchen dining area, which was its own room in that particular house, and back into the kitchen.

We could also detour through a smaller loop from the family room to the sun room and rejoin the big loop right by the kitchen table. Having no dust-collectors around, Karen and I did not worry too much about breaking anything. "Houses are for living in," she would say. What a great mom! Back when all we had were two little boys, she would take them out after a big rain and go stomping in mud puddles. Good times... but I digress.

Bee tag was an open-throttle sprint through the house. It was just as good on a rainy day as it was on sunny days, an all-purpose, all-weather kind of game. Every once in a while, someone would get upset because they were hit too hard with the bee or they were "it" too many times, but MAN what fun!

It was bee-tag kind of days that also saw another favorite family kind of activity. Pile-up on Dad! They would try to wrestle me and get me pinned down.

Nowadays, I have boys that are as big as me. Soon they will be as strong as me. Long gone is the pile-up on Dad thing. I am sure some part of my body would break beyond repair. The girls, too, have matured. They are blossoming into young ladies. They would much rather talk about boys or talk on the phone with their friends than play bee tag.

I don't know. As I sit here in my office staring at the long-forgotten bee I am beginning to wonder – what would they do if I walked in the front door and pelted one of them with the bee. ☺ Then again, perhaps I should go to the gym and get ready for the next round. Perhaps if I am limber enough when I have grandkids, the days of bee-tag will return. I guess I like kids after all.